INTRODUCTION AND PHILOSOPHY

SESSION 1

EVANGELISM *and* **DISCIPLESHIP**

INTERFACING

DR. AARON R. JONES
Foreword by Dr. Timothy M. Hill

Interfacing Evangelism and Discipleship

WORKBOOK

Introduction and Philosophy 1

Dr. Aaron R. Jones

Interfacing Evangelism and Discipleship Workbook

Introduction and Philosophy

Copyright © 2018 by Dr. Aaron R. Jones

Printed in the United States of America

Published by Kingdom Publishing, LLC, Odenton, MD 21113

All rights reserved. No part of this book may be reproduced or transmitted in any form or by any means, electronic or mechanical, including photocopying, recording or by any information storage and retrieval system without written permission from the author, except for the inclusion of brief quotations in a review.

All scripture quotations are from the King James Version of the Bible. Thomas Nelson Publishers, Nashville: Thomas Nelson, Inc. 1972

Editor: Sharon D. Jones

Graphic Designer: Janell McIlwain – JM Virtual Concepts

      Tiara Smith

ISBN: 978-1-947741-15-7

Table of Contents

Interfacing Evangelism and Discipleship Sessions 1

Foreword 3

VISION and OBJECTIVES 5

    Ignite the Fire in the Believer 7

    Inspire the Heart of the Believer 9

    Inform the Mind of the Believer 11

    Illuminate the Call of God 13

PRINCIPLES OF EVANGELISM

    Souls are the Heart of God 18

    Evangelism Teaches the Gospel 19

    A Tool Ordained by God 20

    Evangelism Leads Us to Christ 21

    Evangelism Removes the Blinders 22

PRINCIPLES OF DISCIPLESHIP

    Discipleship is a Tool Ordained by God 30

    Discipleship Establishes and Grows the Gospel in Us 33

    Discipleship is for Those Found in Christ 35

    Discipleship Sharpens Our Vision 37

    Discipleship Explains Truth 39

About the Author 41

Contact Page 43

INTERFACING EVANGELISM AND DISCIPLESHIP

SESSIONS

Session 1—**Introduction and Philosophy**

Session 2—**5 Principles to Encourage Evangelism**

Session 3—**Components of Evangelism**

Session 4—**Bait for Evangelism**

Session 5—**Methodology of Evangelism**

Session 6—**Church Planting Produces Evangelism and Discipleship**

Session 7—**Babes in Christ**

Session 8—**Components of Discipleship**

Session 9—**Evangelism and Discipleship Plan**

Session 10—**Spirit of Forgiveness**

Foreword

When God calls a man of faith and fortitude to a specific purpose in the building of His Kingdom, He uses an individual like Dr. Aaron Jones.

Feeling the urgency of the hour, Dr. Jones has shaped his participation in the FINISH Commitment by emphasizing the merging of evangelism and discipleship strategies to assist churches and individuals in their quests to effectively reach the lost. As Senior Pastor of New Hope Church of God, he is
well-aware of what it takes to affect the Great Commission of our Lord.

Dr. Jones' desire is to instruct others on how to deliberately make an impact on winning souls and then discipling them for powerful Christian service. His all-inclusive approach will intrigue and provide the impetus for those willing to pursue the heart of God.

Interfacing Evangelism and Discipleship will change the course of your outreach!

Dr. Timothy M. Hill
General Overseer
Church of God, Cleveland, Tennessee

Vision and Objectives

Vision

"To build the Kingdom of God by intentional Evangelism and Discipleship of souls."

_____

_____

_____

_____

Objectives

- Ignite the Fire in the Believer

- Inspire the Heart of the Believer

- Inform the Mind of the Believer

- Illuminate the Commandments of God

Objective #1

Ignite the Fire in the Believer

"But ye shall receive power, after that the Holy Ghost is come upon you: and ye shall be witnesses unto me both in Jerusalem, and in all Judaea, and in Samaria, and unto the uttermost part of the earth." Acts 1:8

_____
_____
_____
_____
_____
_____
_____

Additional Notes

Objective #2

Inspire the Heart of the Believer

~ INSPIRE ~

"Looking unto Jesus the author and finisher of our faith; who for the joy that was set before him endured the cross, despising the shame, and is set down at the right hand of the throne of God."

Hebrews 12:2

_____
_____
_____
_____
_____
_____
_____
_____
_____

Additional Notes

Objective #3

Inform the Mind of the Believer

"Let this mind be in you, which was also in Christ Jesus."
Philippians 2:5

_____
_____
_____
_____
_____
_____
_____

Additional Notes

Objective #4

Illuminate the Call of God

- Proverbs 11:30

_____

_____

- Isaiah 6:8

_____

_____

- Isaiah 12:4

_____

_____

- Matthew 28:18-20

_____

_____

- Timothy 2:2

_____
_____

- John 8:31, 32

_____
_____

- 1 Corinthians 11:1

_____
_____

- Matthew 5:16

_____
_____

Additional Notes

PRINCIPLES OF EVANGELISM

Principle #1

Souls are the Heart of God

"The Lord is not slack concerning his promise, as some men count slackness; but is longsuffering to us-ward, not willing that any should perish, but that all should come to repentance."
2 Peter 3:9

_____
_____
_____
_____
_____
_____
_____
_____
_____
_____

Additional Notes

Principle #2

Evangelism Teaches the Gospel

"Teaching them to observe all things whatsoever I have commanded you: and, lo, I am with you always, even unto the end of the world."
Matthew 28:20

_____
_____
_____
_____
_____
_____
_____
_____

Additional Notes

Principle #3

A Tool Ordained by God

"Go ye therefore, and teach all nations, baptizing them in the name of the Father, and of the Son, and of the Holy Ghost."
Matthew 28:19

_____

_____

_____

_____

_____

_____

_____

_____

_____

_____

Additional Notes

Principle #4

Evangelism Leads Us to Christ

"For God so loved the world, that he gave his only begotten Son, that whosoever believeth in him should not perish, but have everlasting life."
John 3:16

_____

_____

_____

_____

_____

_____

_____

_____

_____

_____

Additional Notes

Principle #5

Evangelism Removes the Blinders

"In whom the god of this world hath blinded the minds of them which believe not, lest the light of the glorious gospel of Christ, who is the image of God, should shine unto them."
2 Corinthians 4:4

Additional Notes

PRINCIPLES OF

DISCIPLESHIP

Principle #1

Discipleship is a Tool Ordained by God

"Teaching them to observe all things whatsoever I have commanded you: and, lo, I am with you always, even unto the end of the world."
Matthew 28:20

Additional Notes

Principle #2

Discipleship Establishes and Grows the Gospel in Us

"As newborn babes, desire the sincere milk of the word, that ye may grow thereby."

1 Peter 2:2

_____
_____
_____
_____
_____
_____
_____
_____
_____

Additional Notes

Principle #3

Discipleship is for Those Found in Christ

"But as many as received him, to them gave he power to become the sons of God, even to them that believe on his name."
John 1:12

_____
_____
_____
_____
_____
_____
_____
_____
_____
_____

Additional Notes

Principle #4

Discipleship Sharpens Our Vision

"Iron sharpeneth iron; so a man sharpeneth the countenance of his friend."
Proverbs 27:17

_____
_____
_____
_____
_____
_____
_____
_____
_____
_____
_____
_____

Additional Notes

Principle #5

Discipleship Explains Truth

"Sanctify them through thy truth: thy word is truth."

John 17:17

_____
_____
_____
_____
_____
_____
_____
_____
_____
_____

Additional Notes

❖❖❖❖❖

About the Author

DR. AARON R. JONES serves as Senior Pastor of New Hope Church of God. Under his pastorate is New Hope Kiddie Kollege, Inc (Daycare) and New Hope Community Outreach Services, Inc. Dr. Jones also oversees New Hope Church of God Ghana (2 churches) and New Hope Church of God Uganda (3 churches).

Dr. Jones is an Ordained Bishop with the Church of God denomination and is the DELMARVA-DC District Overseer (16 churches). Dr. Jones serves on DELMARVA-DC's Regional Council, Ministerial Internship Program Board, Urban Ministry Committee, Finance Committee, and Chaplain's Board. He also serves on both the Church of God's International and DELMARVA-DC Ministry to the Military Board. In his local community, Dr. Jones serves as a Chaplain for the Charles County Sheriff Department. He also serves as Board Secretary for the United Ministers Coalition of Southern Maryland, Inc.

Being obedient to 2 Timothy 2:15, "Study to show thyself approved...," Dr. Jones received a Doctorate in Theology and Pastoral Counseling from Life Christian University and a Doctorate in Christian Counseling from American Christian College and Seminary. He is a certified Pastoral Counselor with the International Association of Christian Counseling Professionals. He is a Life and

Pastoral Coach. He is the former Executive Vice President of the National Bible College and Seminary in Fort Washington, Maryland.

Dr. Jones has published ten books and a soul-wining project that provide a biblical foundation for Christian doctrine and discipline. He has recorded a CD entitled, Peace in the Storm. He is the founder and owner of God's Comfort Ministries, LLC, which provides Christian literature, evangelism training, and spiritual guidance. He has appeared live on TCT Network; WATC-TV's Atlanta Live; Babbie's House (hosted by CCM artist Babbie Mason); and In Concert Today on DCTV. He has done radio interviews with Radio One's WYCB's program; The Praise Fest Show; and online with Total Prayze. He was featured on the cover of Change Gospel Magazine and interviewed on Promoting Purpose Magazine.

Dr. Jones not only serves God, but his country as well. He has served over 20 years in the Armed Forces. He is a retired Chaplain with the Army National Guard. He participated in both Operation Noble Eagle (2003) and Operation Iraqi Freedom III (2005).

Dr. Jones is happily married to the former Sharon Russell. He sincerely believes without her love, support, and encouragement, many of his goals would not have been accomplished.

Contact Page

Mailing Address: 150 Post Office Road #1079
Waldorf, Maryland 20604

Website: www.godscomfort.net

Email: drjones@godscomfortmin.net

Facebook: God's Comfort Ministries

Twitter: @GodsComfort_Min

Instagram: @godscomfort_min

GOD'S COMFORT MINISTRIES

God's Comfort Ministries (GCM) provides practical Christian books, teachings, trainings, and coaching to new converts and seasoned believers. GCM provides understanding of the doctrinal principles of the Bible.

Services Provided

Pastoral and Life Coaching

Evangelism and Discipleship Training

Spiritual Guidance

New Author Consultation

Christian Literature